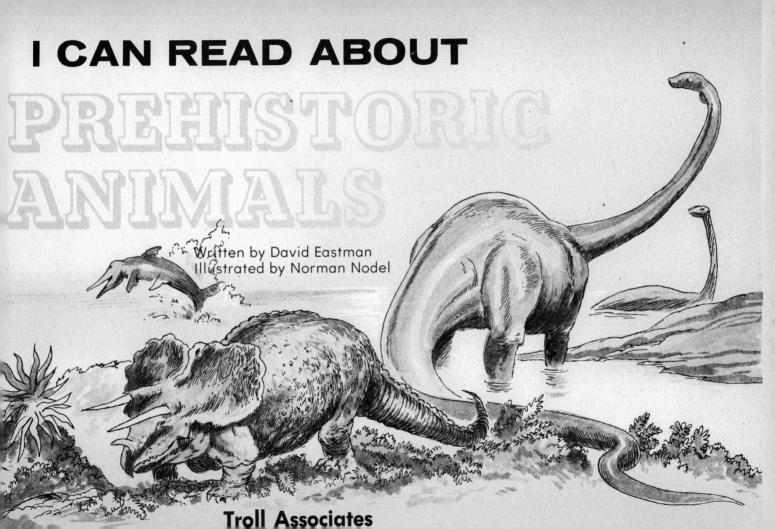

I CAN READ ABOUT
PREHISTORIC ANIMALS

Written by David Eastman
Illustrated by Norman Nodel

Troll Associates

Millions of years ago, dinosaurs and other prehistoric animals lived on earth.
Today, scientists keep learning more about prehistoric animals by
studying fossils.

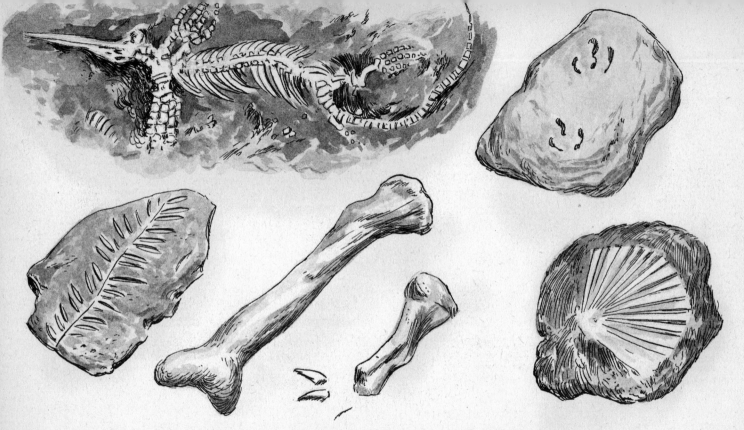

Some fossils are bones that have turned to rock. Some fossils are shells. And some fossils are marks and impressions, like footprints or shellprints, left by prehistoric creatures.

When scientists find fossils, they clean them and number them. If they find bones, they try to fit them together to make a skeleton.

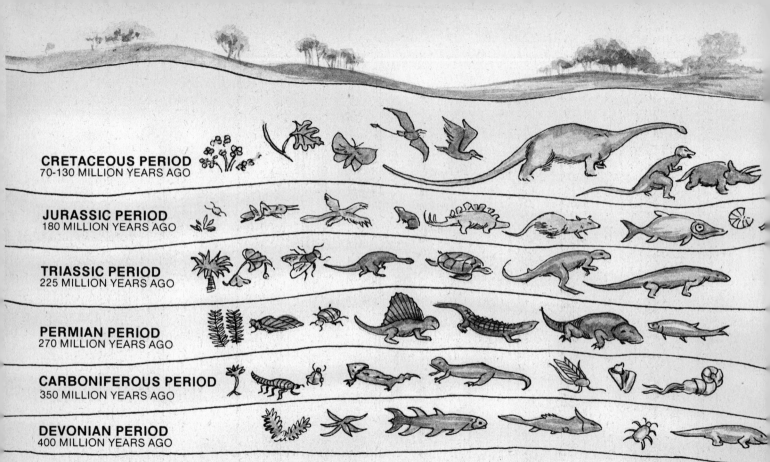

CRETACEOUS PERIOD
70-130 MILLION YEARS AGO

JURASSIC PERIOD
180 MILLION YEARS AGO

TRIASSIC PERIOD
225 MILLION YEARS AGO

PERMIAN PERIOD
270 MILLION YEARS AGO

CARBONIFEROUS PERIOD
350 MILLION YEARS AGO

DEVONIAN PERIOD
400 MILLION YEARS AGO

Scientists divide the earth's history into time periods. Each period has a name.

When a scientist knows how old a fossil is, he knows what time period the animal lived in.

The first animals lived in ancient seas. They were invertebrates (in-VER-tuh-brates). They had no backbone or spine. Jellyfish are invertebrates. They have no backbone or spine.

Sometimes when prehistoric jellyfish died, they left fossil imprints in the sand.

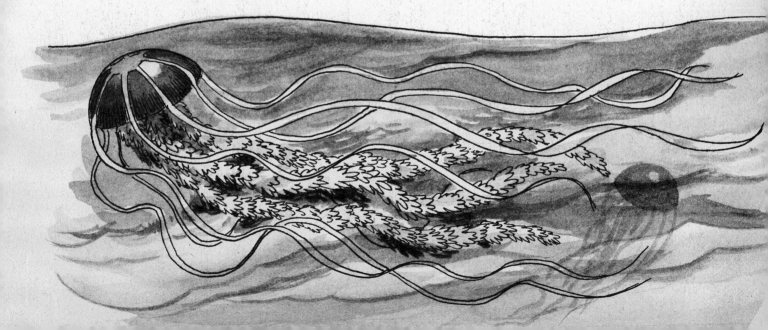

SPONGE

TRILOBITE

SNAIL

There were many tiny animals living in the ancient seas. There were sponges, snails, and shell-covered animals called trilobites (TRY-la-bites). At first, the trilobites were less than an inch long.

GIANT SEA SCORPION

TRILOBITE

Then, after millions of years, the trilobites became larger. They grew to nearly 2 feet long. There were also giant sea scorpions that grew almost 9 feet long.

These prehistoric animals *looked* like fish. They did have backbones, but they did not have jaws. Instead, they had holes or slits for a mouth. They ate small plants and tiny animals.

Some fish-like animals had jaws. Some had armor, or
hard plates of bone, and lived on the bottom of the ocean. Others
had no armor, but could swim very fast.

Some early fish had skeletons made of bone. Others had skeletons made of cartilage (KAR-tih-ledge). Cartilage is soft bone material. Even today, sharks still have skeletons made of cartilage.

Some of the earliest creatures
to live on land were worms and insects
like giant dragonflies.

A fish like the Lobefin (LOBE-fin) used its fins to
crawl out of the water. Gradually, over millions of years,
the lobefins evolved, or changed, into early amphibians (am-FIB-bee-uhns).

Young amphibians are born and live in the water, like fish. But when they are older, amphibians develop lungs, and are able to breathe and live on land. Eryops (EAR-ee-ops) was an amphibian who lived 225 million years ago.

Prehistoric amphibians went through many changes. Some
looked very strange. Scientists think that an animal
like Seymouria (See-MORE-ee-ya) may have been the ancestor of
the early reptiles.

RED SALAMANDER

TORTOISE

FROG

ALLIGATOR

MUD PUPPY
SALAMANDER

SNAKE

Reptiles are born with lungs. They do not
need to be born in water. They have an outside skin made of scales, or hard bony
plates. Snakes, lizards and turtles are modern reptiles.

Most of the early reptiles were not very large. Some
were only one or two feet long. They probably ate insects.
Some had sharp bony points, or spikes, on their heads and backs.

Some reptiles were
meat-eaters who
went after amphibians.

Bradysaurus (Brad-ih-sawr-us)
was a plant-eater. He was 8 feet
long, and had claws on his toes.
He probably used his
claws to dig for
plants.

BRADYSAURUS

Dimetrodon (Dye-MET-ruh-don) had a large jaw and very sharp teeth.
He was a meat-eater. He was 11 feet long, and had a high
3 foot sail on his back.

Different kinds of reptiles developed.
Some looked like snakes with legs. Some looked like
crocodiles. Some looked like lizards. And some
even looked like dinosaurs.

TANYSTROPHEUS

The Age of Dinosaurs began about 200 million years ago. There were many kinds of dinosaurs. Some walked on two feet. Some walked on four feet. Some ate meat, and some ate plants. Not all reptiles that lived in the Age of Dinosaurs were dinosaurs.
Some were reptiles that swam in the water
or flew in the sky.

Brachiosaurus (BRAK-ee-uh-sawr-us) was the heaviest of all the dinosaurs. He weighed 50 tons, and was 80 feet long. Because of his heavy weight, he spent most of his time in the water. It was easier for him to move around in water than on land.

Early meat-eating dinosaurs were not very large.
They walked on their two hind legs, and had short front legs.

COELOPHYSIS

Allosaurus (AL-uh-sawr-us) was big. He was over 35 feet long. He had strong legs, and sharp teeth to hunt even the largest of the plant-eaters.

Tyrannosaurus Rex (Tie-RAN-uh-sawr-us Rex) was the king. He was 47 feet long, and 19 feet high. He had strong hind legs with claws. He had strong jaws, and teeth almost 6 inches long. He could bite through bone. No wonder plant-eaters ran when they saw him.

ALLOSAURUS

TYRANNOSAURUS
REX

Many plant-eaters found safety in the water. The duck-billed
dinosaurs could swim very fast. They had webbed feet and strong
tails. Some had high crests on their heads.

TRACHODON

CORYTHOSAURUS

Iguanodon (Ig-GWAN-uh-don) had hard, pointed claws. He was 16 feet tall and 30 feet long. When he walked, he used his heavy tail to help balance himself.

Some dinosaurs had armor for protection. They had bones, horns, spikes, or hard plates for protection. Triceratops (Tri-SER-a-tops) had three horns and sharp claws. Others like Ankylosaurus (An-KILL-o-sawr-us) had a plate covering, and a tail like a club.

TRICERATOPS

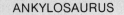

ANKYLOSAURUS

Strange, prehistoric reptiles filled the seas. Huge monsters
hunted their enemies with strong flippers and sharp teeth.
Elasmosaurus (Ee-LAZ-mo-sawr-us) had a neck like a snake and looked
like a sea serpent. He was 40 feet long.

TYLOSAURUS

ELASMOSAURUS

PTERODACTYL

ARCHAEOPTERYX

ICHTHYORNIS

RHAMPHORHYNCHUS

PTERANODON

During the Age of Dinosaurs, new groups of animals developed. Flying reptiles like the Pterodactyl (ter-uh-DAK-til) and Rhamphorhynchus (Ram-for-RINK-us) seemed to have huge bat wings. Pteranodon (ter-AN-uh-don) was another huge monster in the air.

Then another group developed. They were the birds. Like reptiles, the first birds had teeth, but they had feathers instead of scales.

HESPERORNIS

As the earth and its weather changed, a new group of animals appeared. They were the mammals. In the beginning, most were small. Instead of scales, they had fur or hair. Instead of laying eggs, they gave birth to live babies.

OPOSSUM

Unlike reptiles, mammals were warm-blooded. The temperature of their blood did not change with the outside weather.

After the dinosaurs died off, the mammals grew larger and heavier.
Some looked like tiny horses. Some had horns on their noses. Some
looked like strange elephants, only smaller.

Later, mammals began to look more like modern animals. There were huge mastodons (MAS-tuh-dons) with long tusks.

MASTODON

There were huge saber-toothed cats almost as big as modern lions.

Their teeth
were 9 inches long,
and were like strong
knives.

The mammoth lived in Asia, Europe, and North America. He was over 14 feet high.

Scientists know that prehistoric people hunted the mammoth. They probably used spears made of wood, stone or bone.

But prehistoric people were *more* than hunters. On the walls of their caves, they drew pictures of the animals they hunted. In the dawn of history, there was a new creature.

There was someone who could think.
There was someone who could tell a story
for the world to see.

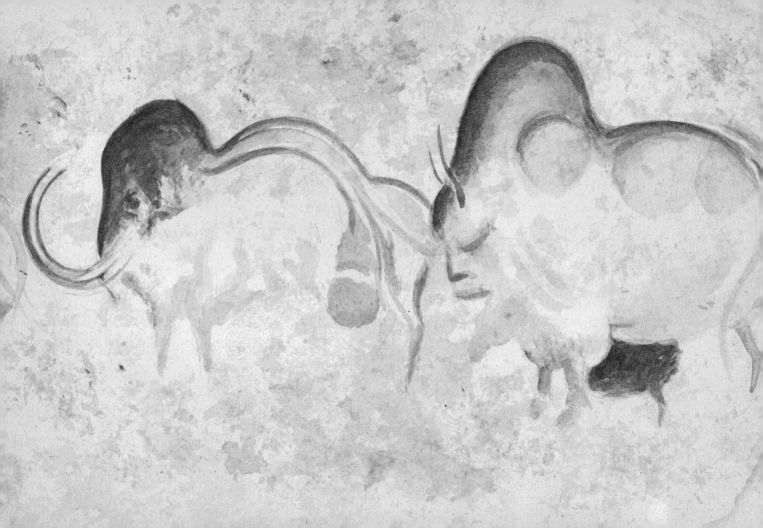